Little Jesus, Did You Know?

By Sandra Finley Doran

AdventSource

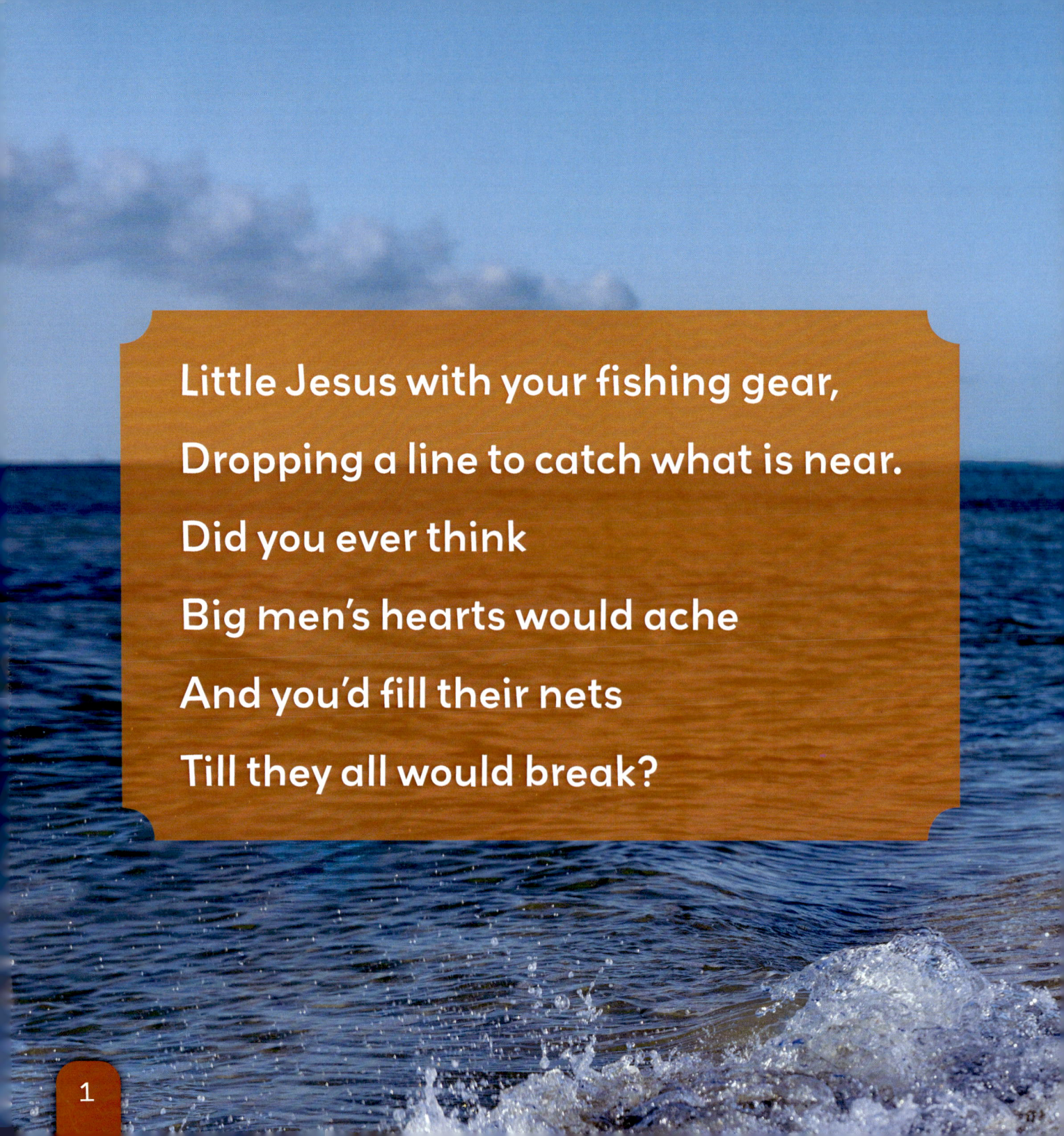

Little Jesus with your fishing gear,

Dropping a line to catch what is near.

Did you ever think

Big men's hearts would ache

And you'd fill their nets

Till they all would break?

Little Jesus by the sea so blue,

Hand in hand, just Dad and you.

Did you know one day

From the sky above

God's voice would call out

You're the Son I love?

Little Jesus singing a song,

Inviting your friends to hum along.

As the chorus flowed sweetly

Filling the air

Did you know the angels

All sang with you there?

Little Jesus with bread and a drink,

Enjoying your meal and time to think.

As you ate your food

Did you ever know

You'd feed five thousand

And make a boy's lunch grow?

Little Jesus helping mom spin thread,
Making the cloth to put on the bed.
As you gazed at the fabric
Of such pure white
Did you imagine the glory
Of your robe so bright?

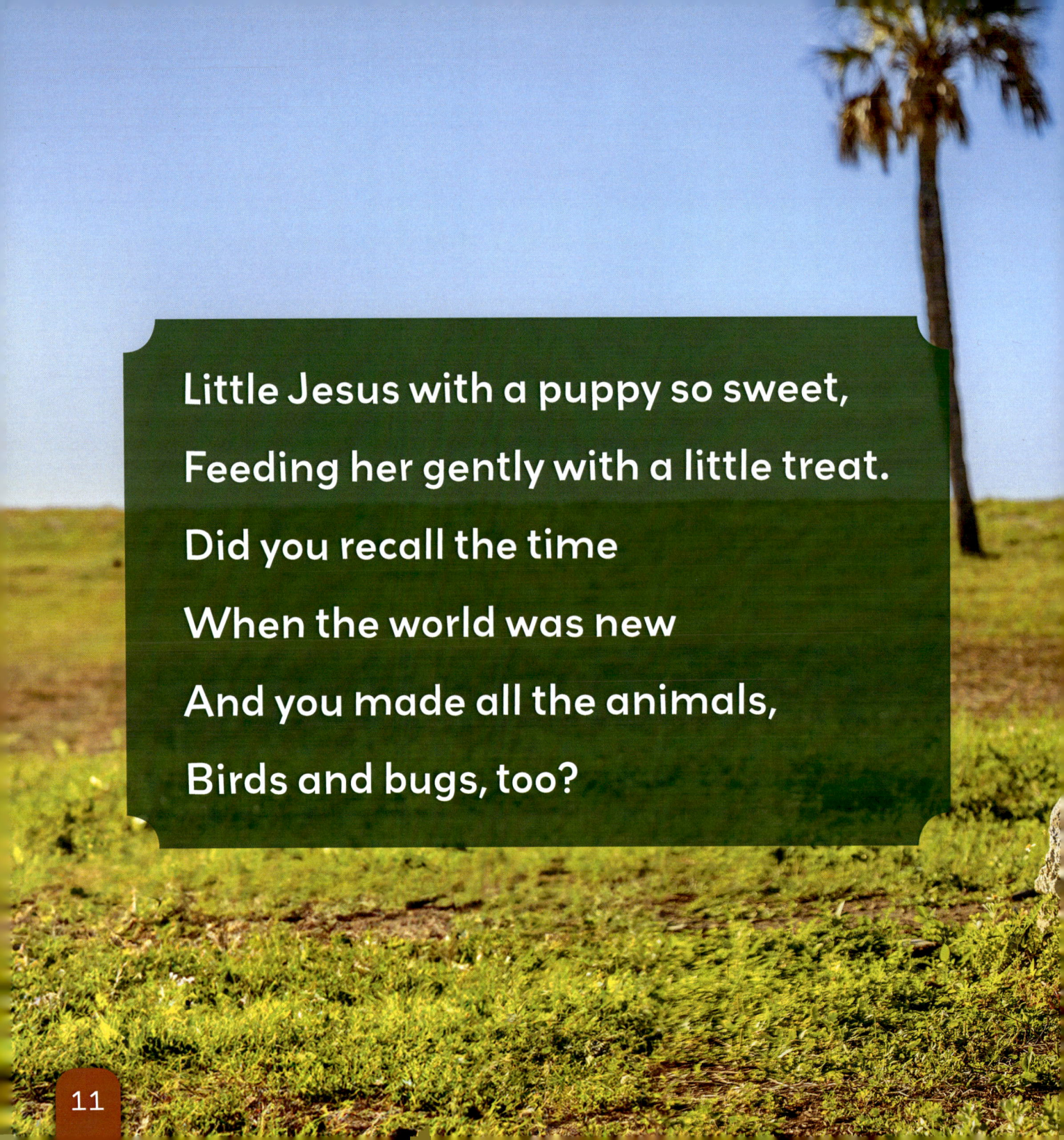

Little Jesus with a puppy so sweet,

Feeding her gently with a little treat.

Did you recall the time

When the world was new

And you made all the animals,

Birds and bugs, too?

Little Jesus sitting with a friend,

Bandaging his knee to help him mend.

Did you see the time

When you'd do so much

Healing so many

With a single touch?

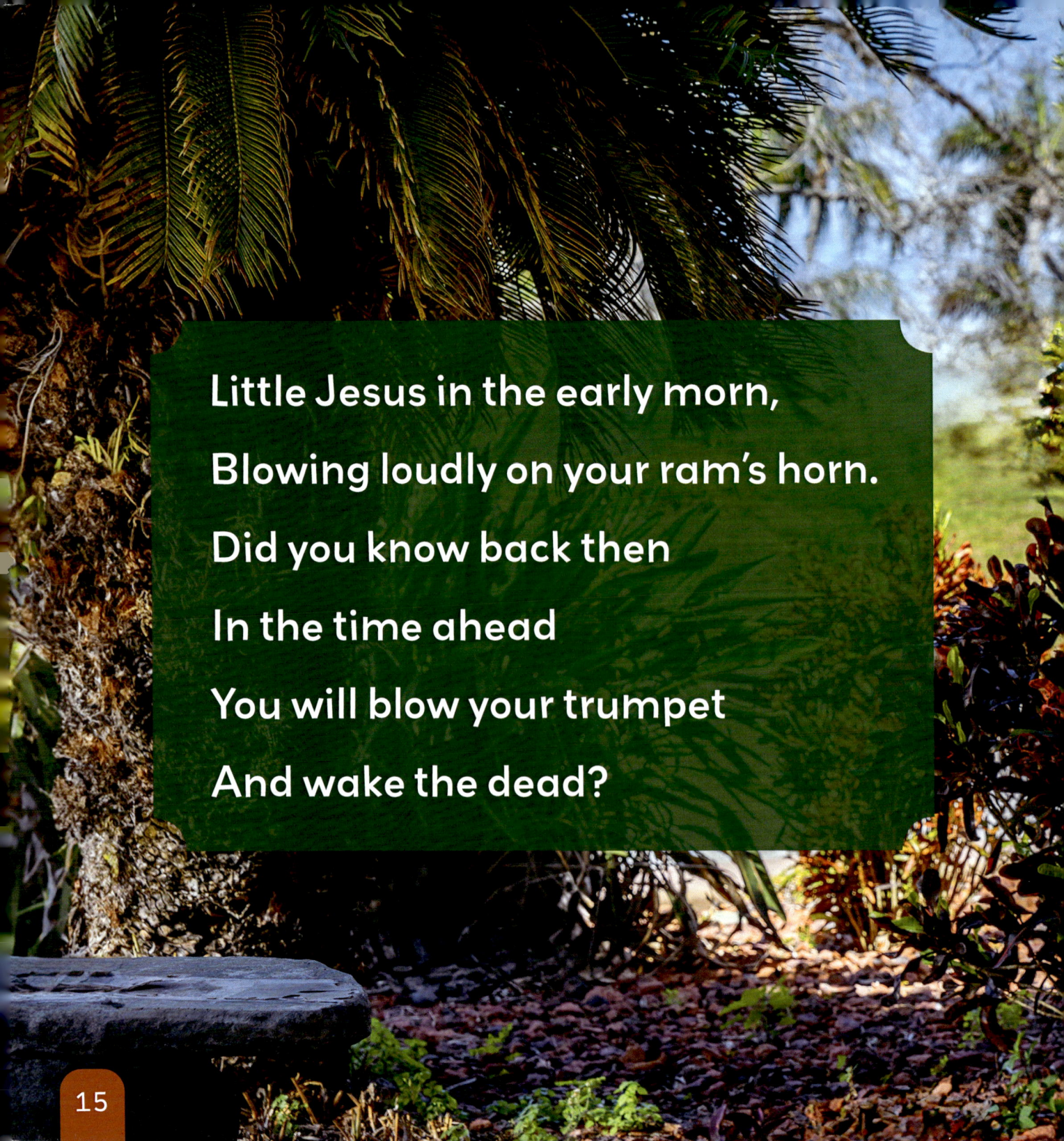

Little Jesus in the early morn,

Blowing loudly on your ram's horn.

Did you know back then

In the time ahead

You will blow your trumpet

And wake the dead?

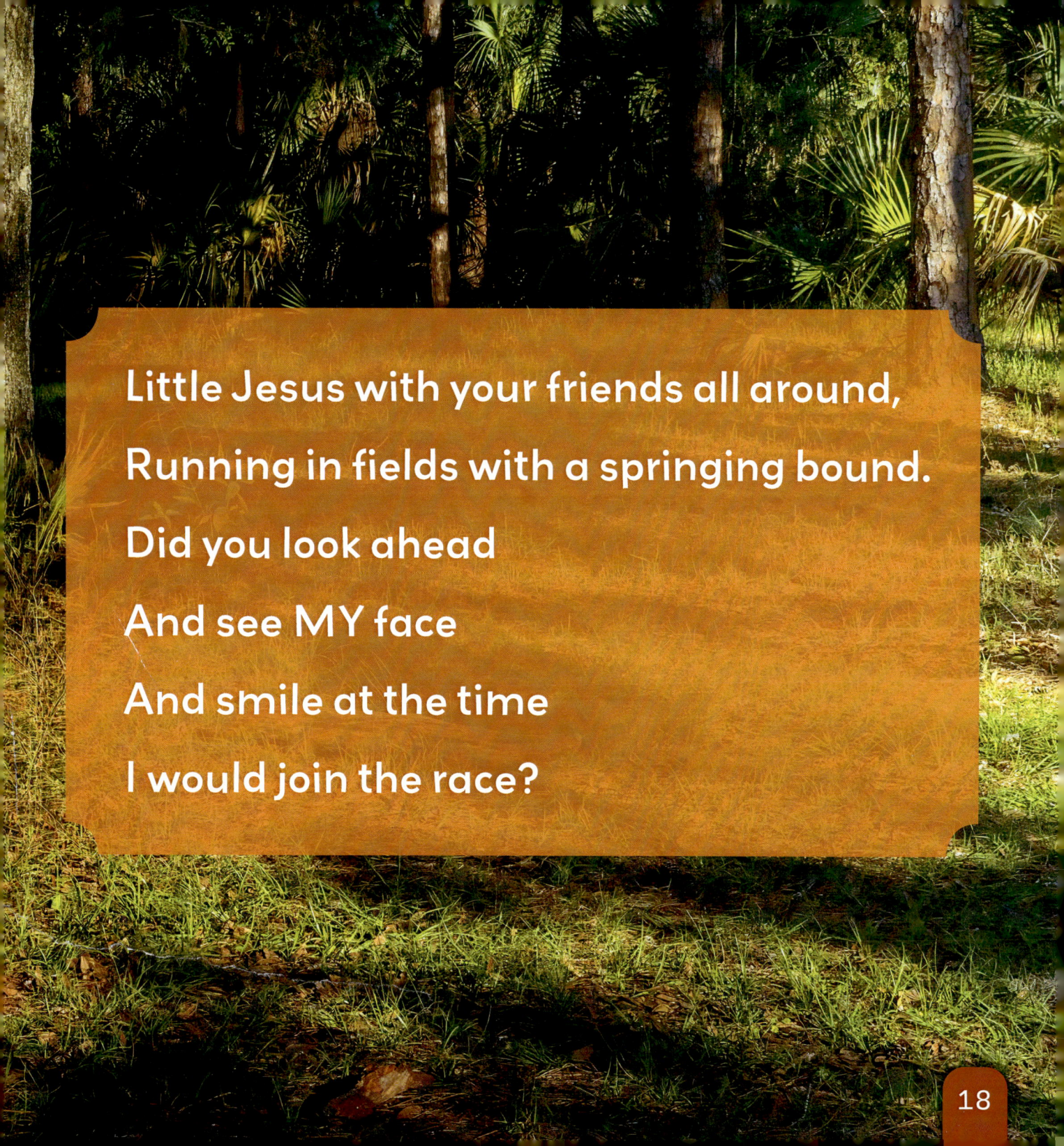

Little Jesus with your friends all around,

Running in fields with a springing bound.

Did you look ahead

And see MY face

And smile at the time

I would join the race?

Bible Story References

Pages 1-2 "fill their nets" - Luke 5:4-11
Pages 3-4 "the Son I love" - Matthew 3:16-17
Pages 5-6 "the angels all sang" - Psalm 148:1-2
Pages 7-8 "feed five thousand" - John 6:1-14
Pages 9-10 "robe so bright" - Matthew 17:1-2
Pages 11-12 "made all the animals" - Genesis 1:20-24
Pages 13-14 "Healing so many" - Matthew 9:35
Pages 15-16 "blow your trumpet" - 1Thessalonians 4:16
Pages 17-18 "friends all around" - John 15:14-15